Books by Mark Strand

POETRY

The Continuous Life 1990
Selected Poems 1980
The Late Hour 1978
The Story of Our Lives 1973
Darker 1970
Reasons for Moving 1968
Sleeping with One Eye Open 1964

PROSE

Mr. and Mrs. Baby 1985
The Monument 1978

TRANSLATIONS

Travelling in the Family 1986
(POEMS BY CARLOS DRUMMOND DE ANDRADE,
WITH THOMAS COLCHIE)
The Owl's Insomnia 1973
(POEMS BY RAFAEL ALBERTI)

ART BOOKS

William Bailey 1987
Art of the Real 1983

FOR CHILDREN

The Planet of Lost Things 1982
The Night Book 1985
Rembrandt Takes a Walk 1986

ANTHOLOGIES

Another Republic (WITH CHARLES SIMIC) 1976
New Poetry of Mexico (WITH OCTAVIO PAZ) 1970
The Contemporary American Poets 1969

The Continuous Life

Mark Strand

The Continuous Life

POEMS

Alfred A. Knopf New York 1992

THIS IS A BORZOI BOOK
PUBLISHED BY ALFRED A. KNOPF, INC.

Published in the United States by Alfred A. Knopf, Inc., New York, and simultaneously in Canada by Random House of Canada Limited, Toronto. Distributed by Random House, Inc., New York.

Some of the poems in this book have appeared previously in the following magazines:

ANTAEUS: "The Continental College of Beauty," "Translation," "From a Lost Diary," "Chekhov: A Sestina" (as "A Little Chekhov"), "The Couple"

ARTICLES: "Cento Virgilianus"

THE BREAD LOAF ANTHOLOGY: "Always," "The Hunchback" (as "Franz"), "The King" (as "Ruins")

GRAND STREET: "Se la Vita E Sventura. . . ," "Reading in Place"

MEMPHIS STATE REVIEW: "Travel"

NEW REPUBLIC: "Velocity Meadows," "Grete Samsa's Letter to H.," "Luminism," "One Winter Night"

THE NEW YORKER: "The Idea," "Orpheus Alone," "A.M.," "Life in the Valley," "The Famous Scene," "Itself Now," "The Empire of Chance," "The Continuous Life," "Danse D'Hiver" (as "A Brief Introduction to Winter")

PLOUGHSHARES: "Narrative Poetry"

POETRY: "To Himself"

SHENANDOAH: "The History of Poetry"

SOUTHERN CALIFORNIA ANTHOLOGY: "The Midnight Club"

THE YALE REVIEW: "Fiction"

WESTERN HUMANITIES REVIEW: "Fear of the Night"

An abridged, limited edition of this title was published by The Windhover Press, Iowa City, in February, 1990.

Library of Congress Cataloging-in-Publication Data

Strand, Mark
The continuous life:poems/by Mark Strand.—1st ed.
p. cm.
ISBN 0-679-73844-4
I. Title.
PS3569.T69C6 1990 90-52947
811'.54—dc20 CIP

I wish to thank the John D. and Catherine T. MacArthur Foundation for a fellowship during the tenure of which a substantial portion of this book was written.
I am grateful to many people who have shown an interest in the poems that make up this book, but I want to mention three whose attention has been especially helpful. They have read and reread all the poems and I have benefitted immeasurably from their comments and advice. They are Jules Strand, Lee Rust Brown, and Nolan Miller. M.S.

Manufactured in the United States of America
First Paperback Edition

T O J U L E S

Contents

Contents

The Continuous Life

The Idea

for Nolan Miller

FOR US, too, there was a wish to possess
Something beyond the world we knew, beyond ourselves,
Beyond our power to imagine, something nevertheless
In which we might see ourselves; and this desire
Came always in passing, in waning light, and in such cold
That ice on the valley's lakes cracked and rolled,
And blowing snow covered what earth we saw,
And scenes from the past, when they surfaced again,
Looked not as they had, but ghostly and white
Among false curves and hidden erasures;
And never once did we feel we were close
Until the night wind said, "Why do this,
Especially now? Go back to the place you belong;"
And there appeared, with its windows glowing, small,
In the distance, in the frozen reaches, a cabin;
And we stood before it, amazed at its being there,
And would have gone forward and opened the door,
And stepped into the glow and warmed ourselves there,
But that it was ours by not being ours,
And should remain empty. That was the idea.

Velocity Meadows

I CAN SAY now that nothing was possible
But leaving the house and standing in front of it, staring
As long as I could into the valley. I knew that a train,
Trailing a scarf of smoke, would arrive, that soon it would rain.
A frieze of clouds lowered a shadow over the town,
And a driving wind flattened the meadows that swept
Beyond the olive trees and banks of hollyhock and rose.
The air smelled sweet, and a girl was waving a stick
At some crows so far away they seemed like flies.
Her mother, wearing a cape and shawl, shielded her eyes.
I wondered from what, since there was no sun. Then someone
Appeared and said, "Look at those clouds forming a wall, those
  crows
Falling out of the sky, those fields, pale green, green-yellow,
Rolling away, and that girl and her mother, waving goodbye."
In a moment the sky was stained with a reddish haze,
And the person beside me was running away. It was dusk,
The lights of the town were coming on, and I saw, dimly at first,
Close to the graveyard bound by rows of cypress bending down,
The girl and her mother, next to each other,
Smoking, grinding their heels into the ground.

A. M.

for Lee Rust Brown

. . . AND HERE the dark infinitive to feel,
Which would endure and have the earth be still
And the star-strewn night pour down the mountains
Into the hissing fields and silent towns until the last
Insomniac turned in, must end, and early risers see
The scarlet clouds break up and golden plumes of smoke
From uniform dark homes turn white, and so on down
To the smallest blade of grass and fallen leaf
Touched by the arriving light. Another day has come,
Another fabulous escape from the damages of night,
So even the gulls, in the ragged circle of their flight,
Above the sea's long lanes that flash and fall, scream
Their approval. How well the sun's rays probe
The rotting carcass of a skate, how well
They show the worms and swarming flies at work,
How well they shine upon the fatal sprawl
Of everything on earth. How well they love us all.

Cento Virgilianus

AND SO, passing under the dome of the great sky,
Driven by storms and heavy seas, we came,
Wondering on what shore of the world
We were cast up. The howling of dogs
Was heard across the twilight,
And over the tombs the rumbling sound
A grassfire makes when it is whipped by the wind;
And later on, from icy courtyards,
The high-pitched wails of women rose
Against the silent golden stars.
At first, we didn't miss the towns we'd started from—
The houses painted pink and green, the swans feeding
Among the river reeds, the showers of summer light
Sweeping over the pasturelands.
So what if we'd hoped to find Apollo here,
Enthroned at last, so what if a cramping cold
Chilled us to the bone. We'd come to a place
Where everything weeps for how the world goes.

Orpheus Alone

IT WAS an adventure much could be made of: a walk
On the shores of the darkest known river,
Among the hooded, shoving crowds, by steaming rocks
And rows of ruined huts half-buried in the muck;
Then to the great court with its marble yard
Whose emptiness gave him the creeps, and to sit there
In the sunken silence of the place and speak
Of what he had lost, what he still possessed of his loss,
And, then, pulling out all the stops, describing her eyes,
Her forehead where the golden light of evening spread,
The curve of her neck, the slope of her shoulders, everything
Down to her thighs and calves, letting the words come,
As if lifted from sleep, to drift upstream,
Against the water's will, where all the condemned
And pointless labor, stunned by his voice's cadence,
Would come to a halt, and even the crazed, dishevelled
Furies, for the first time, would weep, and the soot-filled
Air would clear just enough for her, the lost bride,
To step through the image of herself and be seen in the light.
As everyone knows, this was the first great poem,
Which was followed by days of sitting around
In the houses of friends, with his head back, his eyes

Orpheus Alone

Closed, trying to will her return, but finding
Only himself, again and again, trapped
In the chill of his loss, and, finally,
Without a word, taking off to wander the hills
Outside of town, where he stayed until he had shaken
The image of love and put in its place the world
As he wished it would be, urging its shape and measure
Into speech of such newness that the world was swayed,
And trees suddenly appeared in the bare place
Where he spoke and lifted their limbs and swept
The tender grass with the gowns of their shade,
And stones, weightless for once, came and set themselves there,
And small animals lay in the miraculous fields of grain
And aisles of corn, and slept. The voice of light
Had come forth from the body of fire, and each thing
Rose from its depths and shone as it never had.
And that was the second great poem,
Which no one recalls anymore. The third and greatest
Came into the world as the world, out of the unsayable,
Invisible source of all longing to be; it came
As things come that will perish, to be seen or heard
A while, like the coating of frost or the movement

Orpheus Alone

Of wind, and then no more; it came in the middle of sleep
Like a door to the infinite, and, circled by flame,
Came again at the moment of waking, and, sometimes,
Remote and small, it came as a vision with trees
By a weaving stream, brushing the bank
With their violet shade, with somebody's limbs
Scattered among the matted, mildewed leaves nearby,
With his severed head rolling under the waves,
Breaking the shifting columns of light into a swirl
Of slivers and flecks; it came in a language
Untouched by pity, in lines, lavish and dark,
Where death is reborn and sent into the world as a gift,
So the future, with no voice of its own, nor hope
Of ever becoming more than it will be, might mourn.

Fear of the Night

after Leopardi

ALCETUS: I'm telling you, Melissus,
Looking at the moon just now
Reminds me of a dream I had last night.
I stood at the window, looking at the sky,
And suddenly the moon began to fall.
It came straight at me, getting nearer
And nearer until it crashed
Like a bowl beside the house.
Then it burst into flame, then fizzled
Like a hot coal dropped in water.
It turned black, and the grass was singed.
And that was the way the moon went out.
But there was more to it than that.
When I looked up, I saw an opening in the dark.
It was the hole from which the moon
Had rolled down out of the sky.
I'm telling you, Melissus,
I was scared and still am.

MELISSUS: And why shouldn't you be?
After all, the moon *could* fall at any time.

Fear of the Night

ALCETUS: That's right, look at the stars,
They fall all summer long.

MELISSUS: But there are lots of stars,
And if a few of them fall, so what?
There are thousands left.
But there is only one moon in the sky
And no one has seen it fall but in dreams.

Two Letters

I *Grete Samsa's Letter to H.*

DEAR H., we have been in the new house almost a year, and mother and father have recovered from their ordeal. It is hard to imagine how painful it was for them. As for me, I sleep late as always and practice the violin. But to answer your questions about Gregor: Yes, I admit I am still troubled by what happened to him. Not that I was confident he would wake up the same as he was upon falling asleep. Only the most foolish of us believes we don't change. But who would have thought of going so far! Was he enacting the first stage of a terrible privacy? The last stage of a disfiguring illness? Was he preparing for death in a new and spectacular way? Or was he trying to prove that without inhibitions we become not Berninis or Raphaels but what he became? Perhaps what happened is best seen as a form of religious protest with Gregor allegorizing our hopeless term on earth, except that his interest in spiritual matters could hardly be said to exist. Poor boy! He was after all a poet who, in deference to others, kept his calling a secret. Might we consider his hideous change, then, an indiscretion, a kind of counter-life, a fictive existence in which he became his work? Whatever the case, there were moments when Gregor, already bronzed by the instreaming light of his window, appeared a miraculous monument to himself, both smaller and larger than life. He probably thought that the world, despite its cities, had not begun in earnest, so why not fool around. Alas, I myself have started to feel the onset of something, a sadness perhaps, the dawn of a new season, an existence even. But enough of this. Tell me about yourself and what it is like where you are. Do the leaves ever stop falling? Are the shadows ever anything but long? And the mountains? Can one see them?

2 *Gregor Samsa's Letter to H.*

DEAR H., this interest in me, in what I was for a limited time, is upsetting. I have divined the content of my sister's letter from a privileged perspective, and am astonished that even you should be puzzled by what happened to me. Do we not, if we are lucky, live many lives, assume many masks, and, with death always imminent, do we not keep hoping to be reborn? This is the human condition. We are citizens of one world only when we apply to the next; we are perpetual exiles, living on the outside of what is possible, creating for ourselves the terms of our exclusion, yet hoping to overcome them. Our misery and our happiness are inextricable. So I ask you, why so much attention given to just one life? What of my other lives? Not that I wish to play down my life as an insect. Why should I? It was my strength, my necessity, my triumph. I became what my colleague Raban only toyed with becoming. I gave those who knew me the chance to believe in something that appeared to contradict truth. And yet, I was real, as real as anything. I was irreducible, original, the source of a beautiful and belligerent antinomianism. No amount of disbelief could undo me—undo me into what? My absence? So I could be missed, and thus more present? Oh my dear H., the injustice of life! My best days have been taken from me. I speak to you now from the other side, from yet another exile, changed into a man without meaning or message, living in southern California, getting by as well as I can. How I long for the past, its blend of confusion and terror, its stretches of solitude. To be back in my old room, my old bed, how perfect that seems to me now—now that I feel once more the unknown staring down at the known as if hoping to be recognized into existence. I am speaking, of course, of the work before me. What sadness, what joy.

Chekhov: A Sestina

WHY HIM? He woke up and felt anxious. He was out of sorts, out of character. If only it would go away. Ivashin loved Nadya Vishnyevskaya and was afraid of his love. When the butler told him the old lady had just gone out, but that the young lady was at home, he fumbled in his fur coat and dresscoat pocket, found his card, and said: "Right." But it was not right. Driving from his house in the morning to pay a visit, he thought he was compelled to it by the conventions of society which weighed heavily upon him. But now it was clear that he went to pay calls only because somewhere far away in the depths of his soul, as under a veil, there lay hidden a hope that he would see Nadya, his secret love. And he suddenly felt pitiful, sad, and not a little anxious. In his soul, it seemed to him, it was snowing, and everything was fading away. He was afraid to love Nadya, because he thought he was too old for her, his appearance unattractive, and did not believe that a young woman like her could love a man for his mind or spiritual character. Everything was dim, sharing, he felt, the same blank character. Still, there would rise at times in him something like hope, a glimpse of happiness, of things turning out all right. Then, just as quickly, it would pass away. And he would wonder what had come over him. Why should he, a retired councillor of state, educated, liberal-minded, a well-traveled man; why should he, in other words, be so anxious? Were there not other women with whom he could fall in love? Surely, it was always possible to fall in love. It was possible, moreover, to fall in love without acting out of character. There was absolutely no need for him to be anxious. To be in love, to have a young pretty wife and children of his own, was not a crime or a deception, but his right. Clearly, there was something wrong with him. He wished he were far away . . . But suddenly he hears from somewhere in the house the young officer's spurs jingle and then die away. That instant marked the death of his timid love. And in its vanishing, he felt the seeds of a different sort of melancholy take root within him. Whatever happened now, whatever desolation might be his, it would build character. Yes, he thought, so it is only right. Yes, all is finished, and I'm glad, very glad, yes, and I'm not let down, no, nor am I in any way anxious. No, certainly not anxious. What he had to do now was to get away. But how could he make it look right? How could he have thought he was in love? How out of character! How very unlike him!

To Himself

So you've come to me now without knowing why;
Nor why you sit in the ruby plush of an ugly chair, the sly
Revealing angle of light turning your hair a silver gray;
Nor why you have chosen this moment to set the writing of years
Against the writing of nothing; you who narrowed your eyes,
Peering into the polished air of the hallway mirror, and said
You were mine, all mine; who begged me to write, but always
Of course to you, without ever saying what it was for;
Who used to whisper in my ear only the things
You wanted to hear; who come to me now and say
That it's late, that the trees are bending under the wind,
That night will fall; as if there were something
You wanted to know, but for years had forgotten to ask,
Something to do with sunlight slanting over a table,
An arm rising, a face turning, and far
In the distance a car disappearing over the hill.

Fiction

I THINK of the innocent lives
Of people in novels who know they'll die
But not that the novel will end. How different they are
From us. Here, the moon stares dumbly down,
Through scattered clouds, onto the sleeping town,
And the wind rounds up the fallen leaves,
And somebody—namely me—deep in his chair,
Riffles the pages left, knowing there's not
Much time for the man and woman in the rented room,
For the red light over the door, for the iris
Tossing its shadow against the wall; not much time
For the soldiers under the trees that line
The river, for the wounded being hauled away
To the cities of the interior where they will stay;
The war that raged for years will come to a close,
And so will everything else, except for a presence
Hard to define, a trace, like the scent of grass
After a night of rain or the remains of a voice
That lets us know without spelling it out
Not to despair; if the end is come, it too will pass.

Luminism

AND THOUGH it was brief, and slight, and nothing
To have been held onto so long, I remember it,
As if it had come from within, one of the scenes
The mind sets for itself, night after night, only
To part from, quickly and without warning. Sunlight
Flooded the valley floor and blazed on the town's
Westward facing windows. The streets shimmered like rivers,
And trees, bushes, and clouds were caught in the spill,
And nothing was spared, not the couch we sat on,
Nor the rugs, nor our friends, staring off into space.
Everything drowned in the golden fire. Then Philip
Put down his glass and said: "This hand is just one
In an infinite series of hands. Imagine."
And that was it. The evening dimmed and darkened
Until the western rim of the sky took on
The purple look of a bruise, and everyone stood
And said what a great sunset it had been. This was a while ago,
And it was remarkable, but something else happened then—
A cry, almost beyond our hearing, rose and rose,
As if across time, to touch us as nothing else would,
And so lightly we might live out our lives and not know.
I had no idea what it meant until now.

Life in the Valley

LIKE MANY brilliant notions—easy to understand
But hard to believe—the one about our hating it here
Was put aside and then forgot. Those freakish winds
Over the flaming lake, bearing down, bringing a bright
Electrical dust, an ashen air crowded with leaves—
Fallen, ghostly—shading the valley, filling it with
A rushing sound, were not enough to drive us out.
Nor were those times the faded winter sun
Lowered a frozen half-light over the canyons
And silent storms buried the high resorts
With heavy snows. We simply stayed indoors.
Our friends would say the views—starlight over
The clustered domes and towers, the frigid moon
In the water's glass—were great. And we agreed,
And got to like the sight of iron horses rusting
In the fields, and birds with wings outspread,
Their silver bones glowing at the water's edge,
And far away, huge banks of cloud motionless as lead.

The Continuous Life

WHAT OF the neighborhood homes awash
In a silver light, of children crouched in the bushes,
Watching the grown-ups for signs of surrender,
Signs that the irregular pleasures of moving
From day to day, of being adrift on the swell of duty,
Have run their course? Oh parents, confess
To your little ones the night is a long way off
And your taste for the mundane grows; tell them
Your worship of household chores has barely begun;
Describe the beauty of shovels and rakes, brooms and mops;
Say there will always be cooking and cleaning to do,
That one thing leads to another, which leads to another;
Explain that you live between two great darks, the first
With an ending, the second without one, that the luckiest
Thing is having been born, that you live in a blur
Of hours and days, months and years, and believe
It has meaning, despite the occasional fear
You are slipping away with nothing completed, nothing
To prove you existed. Tell the children to come inside,
That your search goes on for something you lost—a name,
A family album that fell from its own small matter
Into another, a piece of the dark that might have been yours,

You don't really know. Say that each of you tries
To keep busy, learning to lean down close and hear
The careless breathing of earth and feel its available
Languor come over you, wave after wave, sending
Small tremors of love through your brief,
Undeniable selves, into your days, and beyond.

From a Lost Diary

I HAD not begun the great journey I was to undertake. I did not feel like it. At breakfast, I thought of writing to Goethe, but of course did not. I had not met him yet, so could not pretend to be on good terms with him. Would I sit for Raeburn? I turned it over a few times and chose not to. Why should I commit my looks on a particular day to the casual glances of history? I stared a long time at the green fields to the west of the house, and watched with numb fascination the immobility of two spotted cows. Lunch was out of the question, and so was the letter to Wordsworth. I was sure he would not respond. Would I myself write a poem? I had never written one, but decided that nothing would be lost by postponing the experiment. There is so much not to do! Not to visit Blake or Crabb Robinson. Not to write Corot and tell him about the cows. Not to write Turner about my vision of the sun that like a red cry sank and smothered in rippling water until finally far away the water fell into the soundless chasms of an infinite night. What a relief! My mother, hunched over her needlework, urged me to write my sister to whom I had nothing to say. "In many instances it is better and kinder to write nothing than not to write," said she, quoting someone or other. A day so much like the others, why do anything about it? Why even write this down, were it not for my going on record as not having lived. After all, who can believe what is not written down? That I have withdrawn from the abuses of time means little or nothing. I am a place, a place where things come together, then fly apart. Look at the fields disappearing, look at the distant hills, look at the night, the velvety, fragrant night, which has already come, though the sun continues to stand at my door.

Travel

IT MIGHT have been just outside Munich or Rome or on the new road between Santos and São Paulo. It might have been in New York right after the war or in Budapest or Sydney, and now Miami comes to mind. I was always traveling. When she kissed me, when she took off her clothes and begged me to take off mine, we might have been in Prague. When the wind broke tree limbs and shattered windowpanes, we were in Stockholm or almost there. So many places to keep track of. So many sights. It might have been in Philly. I don't know. I can't recall her name, but she sat next to me and put her hand in my pocket, just slipped it in. Later she told me she never spent a night alone, so we climbed into bed and she kept falling asleep. I kept my eyes on the moon. But what I'm talking about happened before Philly, during the dark days when I would lose track of what happened after breakfast. The rain was so heavy, I never opened the blinds. There was nothing to remind me of where I was. I'm not sure, but it might have been in London. She held my hand, then took off her clothes and posed before me, turning this way and that. I think she mentioned Bermuda. I think it was there that she wrapped her legs around me, there in that small room by the sea. I can't be sure. So much has happened. So many days have lost their luster. The miles I've gone keep unraveling. The air is tinged with mist. The cliffs must be closer than they look. I can't be sure. None of the old merriment is here, none of the flash and vigor, none of the pain that kept sending me elsewhere.

Narrative Poetry

YESTERDAY AT the supermarket I overheard a man and a woman discussing narrative poetry. She said: "Perhaps all so-called narrative poems are merely ironic, their events only pointing out how impoverished we are, how, like hopeless utopians, we live for the end. They show that our lives are invalidated by our needs, especially the need to continue. I've come to believe that narrative is born of self-hatred."

He said: "What concerns me is the narrative that provides no coherent framework for measuring temporal or spatial passage, the narrative in which the hero travels, believing he goes forward when in fact he stands still. He becomes the single connective, the embodiment of narrative, its terrible delusion, the nightmare of its own unreality."

I wanted to remind them that the narrative poem takes the place of an absent narrative and is always absorbing the other's absence so it can be named, and, at the same time, relinquishing its own presence to the awful solitudes of forgetfulness. The absent narrative is the one, I wanted to say, in which our fate is written. But they had gone before I could speak.

When I got home my sister was sitting in the living room, waiting for me. I said to her: "You know, Sis, it just occurred to me that some narrative poems move so quickly they cannot be kept up with, and their progress must be imagined. They are the most lifelike and least real."

"Yes," said my sister. "But has it occurred to you that some narrative poems move so slowly we are constantly leaping ahead of them, imagining what they might be? And has it occurred to you that these are written most often in youth?"

Later I remembered the summer in Rome when I became convinced that narratives in which memory plays a part are self-defeating. It was hot, and I realized that memory is a memorial to events that could not sustain themselves into the present, which is why memory is tinged with pity and its music is always a dirge.

Then the phone rang. It was my mother calling to ask what I was doing. I told her I was working on a negative narrative, one that refuses to begin because beginning is meaningless in an infinite universe, and refuses to end for the same reason. It is all a suppressed middle, an unutterable and inexhaustible conjunction. "And, Mom," I said, "it is like the narrative that refuses to mask the essential and universal stillness, and so confines its remarks to what never happens."

Then my mother said: "Your Dad used to talk to me about narrative poetry. He said it was a woman in a long gown who carried flowers. Her hair was red and fell lightly over her shoulders. He said

Narrative Poetry

narrative poetry happened usually in spring and involved a man. The woman would approach her house, wave to the man, and drop her flowers. This," Mom continued, "seemed a sign of narrative poetry's pointlessness. Wherever the woman was, she sowed seeds of disinterest."

"Mom," I ventured, "what we call narrative is simply submission to the predicate's insufferable claims on the future; it furthers continuance, blooms into another predicate. Don't you think that notions of closure rest on our longing for a barren predicate!"

"You're absolutely right," said my mother. "There's no other way to think of it." And she hung up.

Always

for Charles Simic

ALWAYS SO late in the day
In their rumpled clothes, sitting
Around a table lit by a single bulb,
The great forgetters were hard at work.
They tilted their heads to one side, closing their eyes.
Then a house disappeared, and a man in his yard
With all his flowers in a row.
The great forgetters wrinkled their brows.
Then Florida went and San Francisco
Where tugs and barges leave
Small gleaming scars across the Bay.
One of the great forgetters struck a match.
Gone were the harps of beaded lights
That vault the rivers of New York.
Another filled his glass
And that was it for crowds at evening
Under sulphur yellow streetlamps coming on.
And afterwards Bulgaria was gone, and then Japan.
"Where will it stop?" one of them said.
"Such difficult work, pursuing the fate
Of everything known," said another.
"Down to the last stone," said a third,

Always

"And only the cold zero of perfection
Left for the imagination." And gone
Were North and South America,
And gone as well the moon.
One of the great forgetters coughed,
Another yawned, another gazed at the window:
No grass, no trees . . .
The blaze of promise everywhere.

Grotesques

1 *The Hunchback*

IT WAS the middle of the night.
The beauty parlors were closed and the pale moon
  Raced above the water towers.
"Franz," screamed the woman, "take the corpse outside;
  It's impossible to think in here."
"Yes, Ma'am," said the hunchback. When she was alone
  She undid the top two buttons
Of her blouse, crossed the room and played
  The upright in the corner there.
The brief arrangements of her feeling—flawless—
  Bloomed in the October chill.
Cold roses filled the rooms upstairs. Franz,
  Who stood beside the corpse, closed
His eyes and breathed the scented air. If only
  He could have such pleasure every night,
If only the amazing speech of love were not
  So frail and could be caught and held
Forever. Poor Franz. Time was always
  Spinning out of reach. The dark
Trees swayed above the bending blades of grass.

A neighbor's dog, across whose back
Small dots of shadow strayed, had come to sniff
The dead man's matted hair. Far off,
A caterwauling train whizzed past. Franz
Stared for a moment at the dog,
Then quickly checked his watch. It was getting late.
The wind was dying down. Then,
The music stopped and the lights inside the house
Went out. There was an anxious stillness
Everywhere. Franz turned to go. "Come back,"
The woman called. "I'm ready now."
But what about poor Franz? He wouldn't dare
Go back. An hour later, the woman
In a faded robe sat in the kitchen, playing
Solitaire, and Franz lay down
Beside the corpse and slept, unloved, untouched,
In the dull, moon-flooded garden air.

Grotesques

2 *The King*

Not far from the palace
Thc air was filled with haze
That swept, unhindered, into every open place,
And the sea like a blue quilt
Swelled and came apart.
Its blistered scrolls of stuffing littered the shore.
The King was pleased. "Great passions
Seek release," he thought.
Up the road, over the tawny seaside barrens
The sound of a flute caught his ear.
An old hotel, surrounded by arcades
And flanked by towers, lay just ahead.
The water in the swimming pool was clear
And marble gods and goddesses stood around.
Beyond an avenue of trees, half-open books
Were scattered on the lawn for visitors who liked to read.
The King bent down and read a page,
And praised the author, and wiped away a tear.
Farther on, packs of dogs waded in the waves
Of rising heat, or drowsed in the momentary shade

Of a passing cloud. Leafy trees hemmed in
Small tracts of all-white bungalows.
Shafts of heavy sunlight struck the ground.
Beside a house, next to a wood, a woman
In a bathing suit was hanging up her wash.
The King took off his crown and went to her.
Later, climbing from the bed, he thought,
"Have all my royal moments come to this?"
He patted her behind and motored off.
Two men were fishing from a boat, two others
Watching from the shore. The stillness
Of the scene filled him with remorse.
Was it craving for the unknown
That drove him over the countryside?
If a genius finds his subjects far from home,
Why shouldn't a king? He parked the car.
Under the fuss of starlight, under the dusty
Sickle of the moon, he stood alone,
And waited for the birds to sing,
For the wordless tirades of the wind.
He closed his eyes. There was nothing
In the ruins of the night that was not his.

Grotesques

3 *The Couple*

The scene is a midtown station.
    The time is 3 a.m.
Jane is alone on the platform,
    Humming a requiem.

She leans against the tiles.
    She rummages in her purse
For something to ease a headache
    That just keeps getting worse.

She went to a boring party,
    And left without her date.
Now she's alone on the platform,
    And the trains are running late.

The subway station is empty,
    Seedy, sinister, gray.
Enter a well-dressed man
    Slowly heading Jane's way.

The man comes up beside her:
    "Excuse me, my name is John.
I hope I haven't disturbed you.
    If I have, then I'll be gone.

"I had a dream last night
    That I would meet somebody new.
After twenty-four hours of waiting,
    I'm glad she turned out to be you."

Oh where are the winds of morning?
    Oh where is love at first sight?
A man comes out of nowhere.
    Maybe he's Mr. Right.

How does one find the answer,
    If one has waited so long?
A man comes out of nowhere,
    He's probably Mr. Wrong.

Grotesques

Jane imagines the future,
    And almost loses heart.
She sees herself as Europe
    And John as Bonaparte.

They walk to the end of the platform.
    They stumble down to the tracks.
They stand among the wrappers
    And empty cigarette packs.

The wind blows through the tunnel.
    They listen to the sound.
The way it growls and whistles
    Holds them both spellbound.

Jane stares into the dark:
    "It's a wonder sex can be good
When most of the time it comes down to
    Whether one shouldn't or should."

John looks down at his watch:
    "I couldn't agree with you more,
And often it raises the question—
    'What are you saving it for?' "

They kneel beside each other
    As if they were in a trance,
Then Jane lifts up her dress
    And John pulls down his pants.

Everyone knows what happens,
    Or what two people do
When one is on top of the other
    Making a great to-do.

The wind blows through the tunnel
    Trying to find the sky.
Jane is breathing her hardest,
    And John begins to sigh:

Grotesques

"I'm a Princeton professor.
    God knows what drove me to this.
I have a wife and family;
    I've known marital bliss.

"But things were turning humdrum,
    And I felt I was being false.
Every night in our bedroom
    I wished I were someplace else."

What is the weather outside?
    What is the weather within
That drives these two to excess
    And into the arms of sin?

They are the children of Eros.
    They move, but not too fast.
They want to extend their pleasure,
    They want the moment to last.

Grotesques

Too bad they cannot hear us.
Too bad we can't advise.
Fate that brought them together
Has yet another surprise.

Just as they reach the utmost
Peak of their endeavor,
An empty downtown local
Separates them forever.

An empty downtown local
Screams through the grimy air
A couple dies in the subway;
Couples die everywhere.

Se la vita e sventura . . . ?

for Charles Wright

Where was it written that today
I would go to the window and, because it was summer,
Imagine warm air filling the high floating rooms of trees
With the odors of grass and tar, that two crazed bees
Would chase each other around in the shade, that a wall
Of storm clouds would rise in the east,
That today of all days a man out walking would catch his breath
And lean his head back, letting the gilded light
Slide over his upturned face, and that a stranger
Appearing from nowhere, suddenly baring a knife,
Would rip him open from belly to sternum, making his moment
In front of my house his last? Where was it written
That the world, because it was merciful after all, would part
To make room for the blurred shape of the murderer
Fleeing the scene, while the victim, who had already
Slipped to his knees, would feel the heat of his whole being pass
Into a brief, translucent cloud unravelling as it was formed?
Or that a sightless gaze would replace his look of amazement,
That, despite what I guessed was his will to survive, to enter
Once more the unreachable sphere of light, he would continue
To fall, and the neighbors, who had gathered by now,
Would peer into his body's dark and watch him sinking

Se la vita e sventura . . . ?

Into his wound like a fly or a mote, becoming
An infinitesimal part of the night, where the drift
Of dreams and the ruins of stars, having the same fate,
Obeying the same rules, in their descent, are alike?
Where was it written that such a night would spread,
Darkly inscribing itself everywhere, or for that matter, where
Was it written that I would be born into myself again and again,
As I am even now, as everything is at this moment,
And feel the fall of flesh into time, and feel it turn,
Soundlessly, slowly, as if righting itself, into line?

One Winter Night

I SHOWED up at a party of Hollywood stars
Who milled about, quoted their memoirs, and drank.
The prettiest one stepped out of her dress, fell
To her knees and said that only her husband had glimpsed
The shadowy flower of her pudendum, and he was a prince.
A slip of sunlight rode the swell of her breasts
Into the blinding links of her necklace, and crashed.
Out on the lawn, The Platters were singing TWILIGHT TIME.
"Heavenly shades of night are falling . . ." This was a dream.

Later, I went to the window and gazed at a bull, huge and pink,
In a field of snow. Moonlight poured down his back, and the damp
Of his breath spread until he was wreathed in a silver steam.
When he lifted his head, he loosed a bellow that broke and rolled
Like thunder in the rooms below. This, too, was a dream.

Danse d'hiver

WE'VE SEEN them all: the torments of distance,
The sleepy renewals, the fair turning foul,
The line of buildings high in the falling snow,
Down an alley in the center of town
The old gang huddled around a fire,
The new gang warming their hands on each other.

Oh for the moon's displays of pallor.
Oh for the life of the people next door.
The alley points one way but what points the other?
If we should lose ourselves in this weather,
Will anyone know us when we arrive?
Will mother and father feed us or let us go?

The Empire of Chance

ITS TERRAIN is dry and spreads out so you glimpse only bits
At a time; its cities have been known to shine,
But are usually hidden, appearing, suddenly
And by accident, around a bend.
I live near the mountains in a barren
Valley spread with boulders round and red.
I work a field that dims and disappears,
Then circles back to greet me. And after work,
I often sit in the emerald evening air,
My legs stretched out before me,
The collar of my coat turned up,
The wicker chair tilted back,
And wonder what they do up there
In the crystal hills, so cold, so filled
With the lack of what we have down here.
The sound of distant trains, their long
Monotonous whistles, floats down the frozen passes.
And in the dark, under the pressure of starlight,
I dream I'm somewhere else: I hear the sea heaving itself
Upon the shore and the sheer wind
Threading its way through patches of stunted pine
And layers of misted air. And while I strain

The Empire of Chance

To keep that prospect near,
The small night garden behind the house
Sheds its scented moonlit flesh.
When daybreak comes,
The grassless plain beyond my field
Turns grayish pink, the moon's old face
Is pitted and blind, and a few clouds drag
Their skirts of rain.
And in the unshakeable flush
Of sunlight curving down
To take me in, everything spins
Away, beyond my reach, as if my being here
Were some mistake. So the day begins.
The great lake to the west sends up a wall of haze,
The mountains to the south and east a frieze
Of snowy peaks, and the airy reaches
To the north a bank of cold.
Despite its ancient bounds, the empire has no shape.
I work my plot under the screech of gulls
And the sky's deep stare. I work myself
Until I cannot bear my work.
It is the hard truth of what I do.
My shadow shudders in the morning air.

Translation

I

A FEW months ago my four-year-old son surprised me. He was hunched over, polishing my shoes, when he looked up and said, "My translations of Palazzeschi are going poorly."

I quickly withdrew my foot. "Your translations? I didn't know you could translate?"

"You haven't been paying much attention to me lately," he said. "I've been having a terrible time deciding what I want my translations to sound like. The closer I look at them, the less certain I am of how they are to be read or understood. And since I am just a beginning poet, the more like my poems they are, the less likely they are to be any good. I work and work, endlessly changing this or that, hoping by some miracle to arrive at just the right rendering of them in an English beyond my abilities to imagine. Oh, Dad, it's been hard."

The vision of my son struggling over Palazzeschi brought tears to my eyes. "Son," I said, "you should find a young poet to translate, someone your own age, whose poems are no good. Then, if your translations are bad, it won't matter."

2

My son's nursery school teacher came over to see me. "I don't know German," she said, as she unbuttoned her blouse and unsnapped her bra, letting them fall to the floor. "But I feel that I must translate Rilke. None of the translations I've read seem very good. If I pooled them, I'm sure I could come up with something better." She dropped her skirt. "I've heard that Rilke is the German Gerard Manley Hopkins, so I'll keep 'The Wreck of the Deutschland' on my desk as I work. Some of it is bound to rub off. I'm not sure which poems I'll do, but I favor the 'Duino Elegies,' since they are more like my own poems. Of course, I'll be taking German lessons while I work." She took off her panties. "Well, what do you think?" she asked as she stood naked before me.

"You are one of those," I said, "who believes translation is a reading not of the original, but of every available translated text. Why waste money on German lessons, if the actual source of your translation will be already finished translations?" Then, reaching out to shoo a fly from her hair, I said, "Your approach is the editorial one—you edit somebody else's translation until it sounds like yours, bypassing the most important stage in the conversion of one poem to another, which is the initial one of finding rough equivalents, the one which will contain the originality of your reading. Even if you work with someone who knows German, you will be no more than that person's editor, for he will have taken the initial step, and no matter how wisely he rationalizes his choice, it will have been made intuitively or automatically."

"I see your point," she said. "Maybe I should take a stab at Baudelaire."

3

"What's up?" I said to the nursery teacher's husband.

"I have decided not to translate in order to save my marriage," he said. "I'd thought of doing Jorge de Lima's poems, but didn't know how." He dabbed his sweaty upper lip with a crumpled hankie. "I thought perhaps that a translation should sound like a translation, reminding the reader that what he was reading had a prior life in another language and was not conceived in English. But I couldn't bring myself to write in a way that would remind somebody that what he was reading was better before I got hold of it. Dignifying the poem at the cost of the translation seems just as perverse as erasing the original with a translation. Not only that," he said, this time dabbing my upper lip with his hankie, and brushing my cheek with the back of his hand, "but if the dominant poetic idiom of a period determines how a poem is to be translated (and it usually does), it will also determine which poems should be translated. That is, in a period of muttering plain style lyrics, Baroque formulations of a performative sort will not be looked on favorably. So what should the translator do? Should he adopt an antique style? Or would that parody the vitality, ingenuity, and period naturalness of the original? Though de Lima is a twentieth-century poet, his brand of modernism is passé, quite out of keeping with the poetry being written today. So far as I can see, there's nothing to be done with his poems." And with that he disappeared down the street.

4

To get away from all the talk of translation I went camping by myself in southern Utah, and was about to light the campfire when a bare-chested man crawled out from the tent next to mine, stood, and started to file his nails. "You don't know who I am," he said, "but I know who you are."

"Who are you?" I asked.

Translation

"I'm Bob," he said. "I spent the first twenty years of my life in Pôrto Velho, and feel that Manuel Bandeira is the great undiscovered twentieth-century poet, undiscovered, that is, by the English-speaking world. I want to translate him." Then he narrowed his eyes. "I teach Portuguese at Southern Utah State where the need for Portuguese is great since so few people there seem to know it exists. You're not going to like this, but I don't go in for contemporary American poetry and don't see why that should disqualify me from translating. I can always get one of the local poets to look over what I've done. For me, meaning is the important thing."

Stunned by his pencilled-in eyebrows and tiny mustache, I said, a bit unfairly, "You language teachers are all alike. You possess a knowledge of the original language and, perhaps, some knowledge of English, but that's it. The chances are your translations will be word-for-word renderings without the character or feel of poetry. You are the first to declare the impossibility of translating, but you think nothing of minimizing its difficulty." And with that I packed my things, struck the tent, and drove back to Salt Lake City.

Translation

5

I was in the bathtub when Jorge Luis Borges stumbled in the door. "Borges, be careful," I yelled. "The floor is slippery and you are blind." Then, soaping my chest, I said, "Borges, have you ever considered what is implicit in a phrase like 'I translate Apollinaire into English' or 'I translate de la Mare into French,' that we take the highly idiosyncratic work of an individual and render it into a language that belongs to everyone and to no one, a system of meanings sufficiently general to permit not only misunderstandings but to throw into doubt the possibility of permitting anything else?"

"Yes," he said, with an air of resignation.

"Then don't you think," I said, "that the translation of poetry is best left to poets who are in possession of an English they have each made their own, and that language teachers, who feel responsibility to a language not in its modifications but in its monolithic entirety, make the worst translators? Wouldn't it be best to think of translation as a transaction between individual idioms, between, say, the Italian of D'Annunzio and the English of Auden? If we did, we could end irrelevant discussions of who has and who hasn't done a correct translation."

Translation

"Yes," he said, seeming to get excited.

"Say," I said. "If translation is a kind of reading, the assumption or transformation of one personal idiom into another, then shouldn't it be possible to translate work done in one's own language? Shouldn't it be possible to translate Wordsworth or Shelley into Strand?"

"You will discover," said Borges, "that Wordsworth refuses to be translated. It is you who must be translated, who must become, for however long, the author of *The Prelude*. That is what happened to Pierre Menard when he translated Cervantes. He did not want to compose another *Don Quixote*—which would be easy—but *the Don Quixote*. His admirable ambition was to produce pages which would coincide—word for word and line for line—with those of Miguel de Cervantes. The initial method he conceived was relatively simple: to know Spanish well, to re-embrace the Catholic faith, to fight against the Moors and Turks, to forget European history between 1602 and 1918, and to *be* Miguel de Cervantes. To compose *Don Quixote* at the beginning of the seventeenth century was a reasonable, necessary, and perhaps inevitable undertaking; at the beginning of the twentieth century it was almost impossible."

"Not almost impossible," I said, "but absolutely impossible, for in order to translate one must cease to be." I closed my eyes for a second and realized that if I ceased to be, I would never know. "Borges . . ." I was about to tell him that the strength of a style must be measured by its resistance to translation. "Borges . . ." But when I opened my eyes, he, and the text into which he was drawn, had come to an end.

The History of Poetry

OUR MASTERS are gone and if they returned
Who among us would hear them, who would know
The bodily sound of heaven or the heavenly sound
Of the body, endless and vanishing, that tuned
Our days before the wheeling stars
Were stripped of power? The answer is
None of us here. And what does it mean if we see
The moon-glazed mountains and the town with its silent doors
And water towers, and feel like raising our voices
Just a little, or sometimes during late autumn
When the evening flowers a moment over the western range
And we imagine angels rushing down the air's cold steps
To wish us well, if we have lost our will,
And do nothing but doze, half-hearing the sighs
Of this or that breeze drift aimlessly over the failed farms
And wasted gardens? These days when we waken,
Everything shines with the same blue light
That filled our sleep moments before,
So we do nothing but count the trees, the clouds,
The few birds left; then we decide that we shouldn't
Be hard on ourselves, that the past was no better
Than now, for hasn't the enemy always existed,
And wasn't the church of the world already in ruins?

The Continental College of Beauty

WHEN THE Continental College of Beauty opened its doors
We looked down hallways covered with old masters
And into rooms where naked figures lounged on marble floors.
And we were moved, but not enough to stay. We hurried on
Until we reached a courtyard overgrown with weeds.
This moved us, too, but in a moment we were nodding off.
The sun was coming up, a violet haze was lifting from the sea,
Coastal hills were turning red, and several people on the beach
Went up in flames. This was the start of something new.
The flames died down. The sun continued on its way.
And lakes inland, in the first light, flashed their scales,
And mountains cast a blue, cold shade on valley floors,
And distant towns awoke . . . this is what we'd waited for.
How quickly the great unfinished world came into view
When the Continental College of Beauty opened its doors.

The Midnight Club

THE GIFTED have told us for years that they want to be loved
For what they are, that they, in whatever fullness is theirs,
Are perishable in twilight, just like us. So they work all night
In rooms that are cold and webbed with the moon's light;
Sometimes, during the day, they lean on their cars,
And stare into the blistering valley, glassy and golden,
But mainly they sit, hunched in the dark, feet on the floor,
Hands on the table, shirts with a bloodstain over the heart.

The Famous Scene

THE POLISHED scarlets of sunset sink as failure
Darkens the famous scene: nature's portrait of us
On the shore while the flooding sun soils the palms
And wooden walks before the rows of tiny summer homes.
Oh, and the silent birds are hunched in the trees
Or waiting under the eaves, and over there a boat
Cuts through the swell, releasing its coils of steam.
What does it mean to have come here so late?
Shall we know before the night wind strays
Into town, leaving a sea-stale wake, and we close
Our eyes against desire's incoming tides?
Probably not. So let the unsayable have its way.
Let the moon rage and fade, as it will, and the heads
Of Queen Anne's lace bow down in the fields,
And the dark be praised. We shall be off,
Talking aloud to ourselves, repeating the words
That have always been used to describe our fate.

Itself Now

THEY WILL SAY it is feeling or mood, or the world, or the
 sound
The world makes on summer nights while everyone sleeps—
Trees awash with wind, something like that, something
As imprecise. But don't be fooled. The world
Is only a mirror returning its image. They will say
It is about particulars, making a case for this or that,
But it tries only to be itself. The low hills, the freshets,
The long dresses, even the lyre and dulcimer mean nothing,
The music it makes is mainly its own. So far
From what it might be, it always turns into longing,
Spinning itself out for desire's sake, desire for its own end,
One word after another erasing the world and leaving instead
The invisible lines of its calling: Out there, out there.

Reading in Place

IMAGINE A POEM that starts with a couple
Looking into a valley, seeing their house, the lawn
Out back with its wooden chairs, its shady patches of green,
Its wooden fence, and beyond the fence the rippled silver sheen
Of the local pond, its far side a tangle of sumac, crimson
In the fading light. Now imagine somebody reading the poem
And thinking, "I never guessed it would be like this,"
Then slipping it into the back of a book while the oblivious
Couple, feeling nothing is lost, not even the white
Streak of a flicker's tail that catches their eye, nor the slight
Toss of leaves in the wind, shift their gaze to the wooden dome
Of a nearby hill where the violet spread of dusk begins.
But the reader, out for a stroll in the autumn night, with all
The imprisoned sounds of nature dying around him, forgets
Not only the poem, but where he is, and thinks instead
Of a bleak Venetian mirror that hangs in a hall
By a curving stair, and how the stars in the sky's black glass
Sink down and the sea heaves them ashore like foam.
So much is adrift in the ever-opening rooms of elsewhere,
He cannot remember whose house it was, or when he was there.
Now imagine he sits years later under a lamp
And pulls a book from the shelf; the poem drops

To his lap. The couple are crossing a field
On their way home, still feeling that nothing is lost,
That they will continue to live harm-free, sealed
In the twilight's amber weather. But how will the reader know,
Especially now that he puts the poem, without looking,
Back in the book, the book where a poet stares at the sky
And says to a blank page, "Where, where in Heaven am I?"

The End

Not every man knows what he shall sing at the end,
Watching the pier as the ship sails away, or what it will seem like
When he's held by the sea's roar, motionless, there at the end,
Or what he shall hope for once it is clear that he'll never go back.

When the time has passed to prune the rose or caress the cat,
When the sunset torching the lawn and the full moon icing it down
No longer appear, not every man knows what he'll discover instead.
When the weight of the past leans against nothing, and the sky

Is no more than remembered light, and the stories of cirrus
And cumulus come to a close, and all the birds are suspended in flight,
Not every man knows what is waiting for him, or what he shall sing
When the ship he is on slips into darkness, there at the end.

A Note About the Author

Mark Strand was born in Summerside, Prince Edward Island, Canada, and was raised and educated in the United States and South America. He is the author of seven earlier books of poems, the most recent of which was *Selected Poems*, published in 1980. His book of short stories *Mr. and Mrs. Baby* was published in 1985. His translations include *The Owl's Insomnia*, a selection of Rafael Alberti's poems, and *Travelling in the Family*, a selection of Carlos Drummond de Andrade's poems, edited in collaboration with Thomas Colchie. He has written several children's books, and edited several anthologies, including *Another Republic*, which he co-edited with Charles Simic. He has published numerous articles and essays on painting and photography, and in 1987 his book on William Bailey was published. He has been the recipient of fellowships from the Ingram Merrill, Rockefeller and Guggenheim Foundations and from the National Endowment for the Arts. In 1979 he was awarded the Fellowship of the Academy of American Poets, and in 1987 he received a John D. and Catherine T. MacArthur Fellowship. He has taught at many colleges and universities, and since 1981 has been a professor of English at the University of Utah. In 1990 he was chosen by the Librarian of Congress to be Poet Laureate of the United States. He lives in Salt Lake City with his wife and son.

A Note on the Type

This book was set on the Linotype in Janson, a recutting made direct from type cast from matrices long thought to have been made by the Dutchman Anton Janson, who was a practicing type founder in Leipzig during the years 1668–1687. However, it has been conclusively demonstrated that these types are actually the work of Nicholas Kis (1650–1702), a Hungarian, who most probably learned his trade from the master Dutch type founder Dirk Voskens. The type is an excellent example of the influential and sturdy Dutch types that prevailed in England up to the time William Caslon developed his own incomparable designs from them.

Composition by Heritage Printers, Inc.,
Charlotte, North Carolina
Printed and bound by Halliday Lithographers
West Hanover, Massachusetts
Designed by Harry Ford